GORILLAS

GORILLAS

PETER MURRAY
THE CHILD'S WORLD

Early one morning, in a clearing deep in the African rainforest, a family is getting ready to start a new day. The father is the first to wake up. He yawns, rubs his eyes, and rolls out of bed. His bed is made of branches and leaves. He pulls up a root and takes a big, noisy bite.

A few feet away, a baby hears her father eating. She tugs at her mother's long hair. The mother wakes up and hugs the baby to her breast. All around them, other family members begin to move around, making soft hooting noises. The gorilla family is awake.

The father gorilla is the biggest gorilla in the group. He weighs 400 pounds, is six feet tall, and is twenty-eight years old. For a gorilla, that's old! Most wild gorillas don't live that long. The hair on his back has turned a beautiful silvery gray. For this reason, older male gorillas are called *silverbacks*.

The other gorillas in the group are females and young males. Their hair is solid black, and they are much smaller than their male leader. When the big silverback moves off through the forest, the other gorillas follow him. The silverback is their leader.

Gorillas walk on all fours, using the knuckles of their hands and the soles of their feet. This "knuckle-walking" is how gorillas prefer to travel. Humans are the only mammals that walk on two feet.

Today the silverback is taking his family out to dinner. They are going to look for food in the rainforest. Gorillas spend much of their time eating. A big gorilla can eat about sixty pounds of food a day! Fortunately, there is a lot of food in the rainforest. Gorillas enjoy eating fruit, roots, tree bark, bamboo shoots, vines, leaves, and even grass.

Humans, chimpanzees, monkeys, and gorillas are all members of the *primate* group of animals. Primates have large brains and hands that can grasp. Humans have the largest brains of any primates, but gorillas are not far behind!

Gorillas communicate with each other by using sounds and gestures. One captive gorilla named Koko has even learned to "talk" to humans. Koko uses American Sign Language to communicate with her keepers. Scientists disagree on how intelligent gorillas really are, but all agree that they are among the smartest animals on earth.

When the silverback finds a patch of tasty plants, the family stops to feed. Using their flexible hands, the gorillas pull leaves from branches and yank roots from the ground. They chew and grind the food with their powerful teeth. When the silverback tires of one food, he leads his band through the jungle until they find some other food. Since gorillas spend about one-third of their lives eating, they like variety in their diet. Sometimes they even eat certain types of dirt!

When everyone has had enough to eat, it's time to settle down for an afternoon nap. The silverback decides when and where to rest. The adult gorillas spread themselves out on the ground and snooze for an hour or two. While the adults sleep, the young gorillas wrestle and play. They climb trees and play gorilla versions of "tag" and "follow the leader." Sometimes they get excited and run right over the adults!

Three types of gorillas live in Africa. Western lowland gorillas live in the warm rainforests of Cameroon, Gabon, and Congo Brazzaville. Eastern lowland gorillas live in eastern Zaire. The rare mountain gorillas live in a small, mountainous region along the border of Zaire, Uganda, and Rwanda. All of these gorillas are members of the same species and have similar habits. However, mountain gorillas live in a cooler habitat and have longer hair to keep them warm.

Gorillas live in family groups of ten to thirty individuals. The silverback's job is to lead the group and protect it from danger. If a group is approached by strange gorillas or by humans, the silverback will drive them away by roaring, beating his chest, and ripping the branches from trees and throwing them. In gorilla talk, this means "Go away!"

If the visitors don't take the hint and leave, the silverback might charge! All he really wants to do is scare the intruders away, but if he thinks his group is in danger, he might attack.

Although there may be other males in a family group, the silverback is the only one who mates with the females. He is the father of all the baby gorillas in the group.

When a baby is born, it weighs only about four pounds. The other gorillas are curious and want to meet the new baby. However, the mother won't let anyone touch her tiny, helpless baby—not even the silverback! The baby spends the first days of its life clinging to its mother, holding on to her hair with its strong little hands. When the baby is a few weeks old, the mother introduces it to the other gorillas.

Baby gorillas grow more quickly than humans. In three months the baby is already crawling. By six months, it is climbing trees! The baby stays close to its mother for the first three years of its life.

Gorillas look fierce, but they are gentle creatures. The young are a very important part of gorilla life. Adult gorillas are very gentle and patient with their offspring. Even the big silverback enjoys playing with the young gorillas.

Like many other rainforest creatures, gorillas are endangered by human activities. Farmers clear the rainforest and use the land to grow crops. As the rainforest shrinks, fewer and fewer gorillas are able to survive. Gorillas need space to roam and food to eat. They are shy creatures, and they do not like to live near human settlements. Colds and other human diseases can be deadly to gorillas. Contact with people can make an entire family of gorillas sick.

Mountain gorillas are nearly extinct due to poaching and loss of habitat. The few hundred that remain live in national parks, where they are protected from hunters. Even so, poaching continues. Gorillas are killed for their hands, skulls, and teeth, which are sold as souvenirs. Baby gorillas are captured and sold illegally to zoos or animal collectors. Because adult gorillas try to protect their young, poachers sometimes must kill several adult gorillas to capture one baby.

Gorillas are one of our closest animal relatives. Sometimes they seem almost human! They live in family groups, take care of one another, and communicate with sounds and gestures. Gorillas are highly intelligent, and their hands look very much like ours.

When you look into a gorilla's eyes, you have to wonder what it is thinking. Maybe it thinks you are another gorilla. Maybe it is wondering what happened to all your hair!

INDEX

PHOTO RESEARCH
Charles Rotter / Archipelago Productions

PHOTO CREDITS
COMSTOCK / Boyd Norton: 2, 24
E. R. Degginger: 4, 17
Len Rue, Jr.: 7, 21
Ron Kimball: front cover, 13, 18, 27, 28
Walt Anderson: 8, 11, 14, 22, 31

Library of Congress Cataloging-in-Publication Data
Murray, Peter, 1952 Sept. 29-
Gorillas / Peter Murray.
p. cm.
Summary: Reveals the physical characteristics,
behavior, family structure, and life cycle of the gorilla.
ISBN 1-56766-020-7

1. Gorilla--Juvenile literature.   [1. Gorilla.]   I. Title.
QL737.P96M875   1993   93-13649
599.88'46--dc20

Distributed to schools and libraries in the United States by:
ENCYCLOPAEDIA BRITANNICA EDUCATIONAL CORP.
310 South Michigan Avenue
Chicago, Illinois 60604

NATURE FILES

ANIMAL GROUPINGS

Anita Ganeri

Heinemann
LIBRARY

CONTENTS

The Portuguese man-of-war belongs to a group of sea animals called coelenterates. It is related to jellyfish, corals and sea anemones. It floats near the surface of the sea.

Spiders are arachnids, the group that also includes ticks and mites. All share certain features, they have eight legs and two body segments.

INTRODUCTION

An astonishing variety of animals live on planet Earth. Animals come in a huge range of shapes and sizes, from tiny spiders to giant tortoises, and from fragile jellyfish to great apes. Millions of species are known to science, and there may be millions more yet to find. To make it easier to identify different animals, scientists divide them into groups, based on their main characteristics and shared features.

Tortoises, turtles, snakes, lizards, alligators and crocodiles are all species of reptiles, an ancient group of animals.

These ring-tailed lemurs are mammals, the group of animals to which human beings belong. Lemurs are part of a group of mammals called primates, along with apes, monkeys and human beings.

There are about 1,500,000 species of animals. These are the species which scientists have named and studied. However the true number of animals living on Earth may be ten times greater than that.

ANIMAL GROUPS

To make it easier to pick out an individual species of animal, scientists divide animals into groups, based on their shared features. This way of grouping is known as taxonomy, or classification. Each species is given a scientific Latin name. The same animal can have several different common names – the crane fly is also called a daddy long legs – but only one scientific name.

Amazing FACT

A Swedish botanist, Carl von Linné (1707–1778), devised the modern system of classification and introduced the use of Latin names. He even Latinized his own name to become Carolus Linnaeus.

Carolus Linnaeus.

ANIMAL CLASSIFICATION

The largest group in classification is the animal kingdom which includes all animals. This group is broken down into smaller and smaller groups, based on similarities between members of each group and differences between them and the animals in other groups. First the kingdom is divided into phyla (singular: phylum). Each phylum is split into classes, and each class into orders. Each order is divided into families, which each contain several genera (singular: genus). Each genus is split into species. Below you can see how classification works for a polar bear.

Kingdom: Animalia (Animals)
Phylum: Chordata (Chordates)
Sub-phylum: Vertebrata (Vertebrates)
Class: Mammalia (Mammals)
Order: Carnivora (Carnivores)
Family: Ursidae (Bears)
Genus: Ursus
Species: Ursus maritimus (Polar bear)

INVERTEBRATES

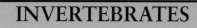

SPONGES

JELLYFISH, ANEMONES AND CORALS

EARTHWORMS AND OTHER TRUE WORMS

SNAILS, SQUIDS AND OTHER MOLLUSCS

STARFISH AND SEA-URCHINS

ARTHROPODS

CRABS, LOBSTERS AND OTHER CRUSTACEANS

CENTIPEDES

MILLIPEDES

INSECTS

SPIDERS AND SCORPIONS

VERTEBRATES

FISH
JAWLESS FISH, SHARKS AND RAYS, BONY FISH

AMPHIBIANS
FROGS AND TOADS, NEWTS AND SALAMANDERS, CAECILIANS

REPTILES
TORTOISES AND TURTLES, TUATARAS, SNAKES, LIZARDS, CROCODILES

BIRDS
OSTRICHES, RHEAS, CASSOWARIES AND EMUS, KIWIS, TINAMOUS, PENGUINS, DIVERS, GREBES, ALBATROSSES AND PETRELS, PELICANS, HERONS, FLAMINGOES, WATERFOWL, BIRDS OF PREY, GAMEBIRDS, CRANES, WADERS, GULLS AND AUKS, PIGEONS, SANDGROUSE, PARROTS, CUCKOOS, OWLS, NIGHTJARS AND FROGMOUTHS, HUMMINGBIRDS AND SWIFTS, MOUSEBIRDS, TROGONS, KINGFISHERS, WOODPECKERS AND TOUCANS, PASSERINES

MAMMALS
EGG-LAYING MAMMALS, MARSUPIALS, INSECTIVORES, BATS, FLYING LEMURS, ELEPHANT-SHREWS, TREE SHREWS, PRIMATES, ANTEATERS, PANGOLINS, RABBITS AND HARES, RODENTS, WHALES AND DOLPHINS, CARNIVORES, SEALS AND SEA LIONS, ELEPHANTS, AARDVARK, HYRAXES, DUGONG AND MANATEES, HOOFED MAMMALS

The main difference between plants and animals lies in how they obtain their food. Most plants make their own food by photosynthesis but animals must move to find food. An animal's body is made up of cells, tissues, organs and organ systems. A simple way of dividing animals (left) is by separating them into two groups: invertebrates (animals without a backbone) and vertebrates (animals with a backbone). *To find out more about invertebrates see pages 8–17 and for more about vertebrates see pages 18–29.*

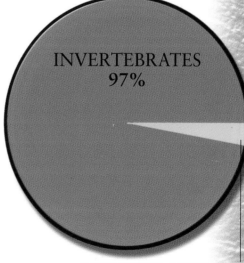

INVERTEBRATES 97%

VERTEBRATES 3%

With more than 950,000 species, there are far more invertebrates than vertebrates. About 97 per cent of all animals are invertebrates.

SIMPLE CREATURES

Invertebrates do not have backbones or bony skeletons inside their bodies. Instead, some invertebrates grow hard shells or cases, called exoskeletons, to support and protect their bodies. There are many groups of invertebrates, based on the features they share.

SIMPLE SPONGES

Sponges are very simple animals. Their bodies are made of layers of cells, strengthened by tough fibres. Adult sponges fix themselves to rocks and feed on tiny particles floating past.

Huge and spectacular coral reefs are built by coral polyps. These tiny animals are related to jellyfish and sea anemones.

WEIRD WORMS

All worms share a long, thin body shape but there are many different kinds. Annelid worms, such as earthworms and leeches, have bodies divided into segments. In earthworms, each segment has a pair of bristles which help the worm to move. Leeches feed on blood. They have suckers at each end of their bodies for gripping their prey.

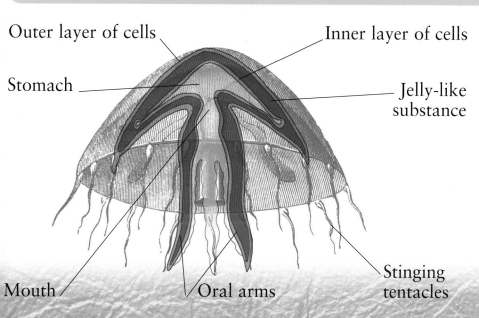

Earthworms usually live underground and feed on soil and dead leaves.

JELLYFISH BODY PLAN

Outer layer of cells

Inner layer of cells

Stomach

Jelly-like substance

Mouth

Oral arms

Stinging tentacles

Jellyfish, corals and sea anemones belong to a group of invertebrates called coelenterates. Their soft, circular bodies are made up of two layers of cells, with a jelly-like layer in between. Their mouths are surrounded by rows of stinging tentacles which are used for catching food.

9

SHELLS AND SPINES

Molluscs and echinoderms are groups of invertebrates that use tough shells or spines to protect their soft bodies. Molluscs make up the second largest group of invertebrates. Echinoderms live up to their name which means 'spiny skinned'.

MARVELLOUS MOLLUSCS

There are about 75,000 species of molluscs, divided into smaller groups. Slugs and snails are gastropods (see below). Scallops and clams are bivalves, with two parts to their shells.

Not all molluscs have protective shells. The blue-ringed octopus defends itself with a painful and poisonous bite.

SNAIL BODY PLAN

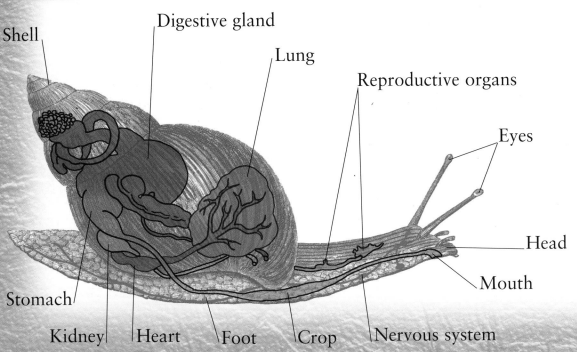

Shell
Digestive gland
Lung
Reproductive organs
Eyes
Head
Mouth
Stomach
Kidney
Heart
Foot
Crop
Nervous system

Although molluscs vary widely, their bodies follow the same basic plan. The main part of the body contains the organs and is often protected by a shell. Below, there is a muscular foot, used for walking or swimming. In snails, the foot is wide and flat and sticks out from under the shell.

SPINY SKINS

Starfish, sea urchins and brittlestars belong to a group of invertebrates, called echinoderms. Their bodies are arranged in five parts, around a central mouth, and are covered in spines. Echinoderms move around on thousands of tiny, hollow tentacles, called tube feet, which are also used for breathing and feeding.

Many starfish have five arms, although some can have as many as 40. If one arm is damaged, a starfish grows another one. Sometimes, a whole starfish can grow from a small piece of arm.

Amazing FACT

The Atlantic giant squid is a huge mollusc that can measure over 16 metres long and weigh two tonnes. Each eye is twice as big as a dinner plate. However, the largest invertebrate is the colossal squid, which has razor-sharp hooks on its tentacles.

Atlantic giant squid.

Giant clams are bivalve molluscs. Their shells are made in two halves, joined by an elastic hinge. A giant clam shell can measure over a metre across.

11

AWESOME ARTHROPODS

Insects, spiders, crabs, lobsters, millipedes and mites all belong to the biggest group of invertebrates on Earth – the arthropods. Four out of every five animals alive are arthropods.

CRUSTACEANS

Most crustaceans live in the sea. Only land crabs and woodlice have adapted to life on land. A crustacean's soft body is covered in a hard shell which cannot stretch as the animal grows. So the shell is shed and a new, larger shell grows.

Instead of pincers, spiny lobsters have huge antennae, to scare off hungry fish.

LOBSTER BODY PLAN

The name arthropod means 'jointed legs'. Like this lobster, all arthropods have legs that bend at joints and bodies divided into segments. A lobster has ten pairs of legs. Its front pair are huge pincers for grabbing and crushing food. Its other legs have claws for walking and gripping rocks.

Brain

Stomach

Reproductive organs

Heart

Antennule

Intestine

Segmented body

Bladder

Pincers (1st pair of legs)

Gills

3rd pair of legs

2nd pair of legs

4th pair of legs

5th pair of legs

Antennae

Amazing FACT

The largest of all crustaceans is the Japanese spider crab. It is also called the stilt crab because of its very long, spindly legs. The biggest crab on record had a legspan of 3.7 metres, measured across its front claws.

Japanese spider crab.

MANY LEGS

Centipedes and millipedes belong to a group of arthropods called myriapods, or 'many legs'. Both have long, slim bodies, divided into segments. But centipedes have one pair of legs on each segment, while millipedes have two. Centipedes are fierce hunters. Millipedes are harmless plant-eaters.

The record number of legs for a millipede (above) is 750 legs (375 pairs). They cannot move very fast. If danger threatens, many species roll into a ball.

Centipedes like to lurk in dark, damp places under bark, logs and stones. They come out at night to hunt for prey. Centipedes can grow over 30 cm long.

13

There are more species of insects than all other kinds of animals put together. So far, at least a million species have been identified, but many millions more are still to be discovered.

INSECT GROUPS

The vast and varied group of insects includes beetles, butterflies, ants, bees, grasshoppers, flies and weevils. Insects live all over the world, from the icy poles to the driest deserts. They successfully adapt their lifestyles to changing conditions. For example, they can eat almost anything.

Most insects, such as the cockchafer (above), are small. But their ability to fly has allowed them to travel long distances to settle in new habitats and escape from enemies.

INSECT BODY PLAN

Like all arthropods, insects have segmented bodies and jointed legs. Their bodies are divided into three parts – the head, thorax and abdomen. Their wings and six legs are attached to their thorax. An insect's head has two compound eyes and a pair of antennae. Its body is covered in a tough casing called an exoskeleton, which has small breathing holes called spiracles.

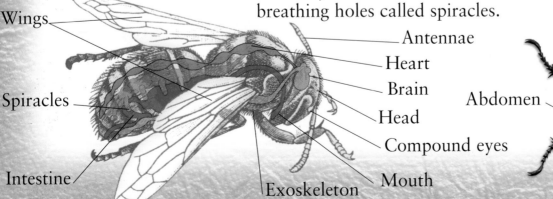

Wings

Spiracles

Intestine

Antennae

Heart

Brain

Head

Compound eyes

Exoskeleton

Mouth

Thorax   Head

Abdomen

Six legs

LIFE CYCLES

Many insects go through amazing changes as they grow and turn into adults. This process is called metamorphosis. A butterfly, for example, lays eggs that hatch into larvae called caterpillars. A caterpillar feeds and grows rapidly before it turns into a chrysalis or pupa. Inside the pupa, its body breaks down and reforms as an adult butterfly.

Amazing FACT

A stick insect from the rainforests of South East Asia is the world's longest insect. With its legs, it can grow as long as your arm. Stick insects are masters of disguise to avoid being eaten. Their slim bodies look like twigs or stems. Even their eggs look like plant seeds.

Stick insects copy rigid twigs.

A pupa splits open as a butterfly struggles out. Its wings are soft and crumpled. They will expand and harden as blood starts to flow through them.

Some insects, such as ants and wasps, live in huge groups or colonies. In a honeybee swarm, each individual bee has its own particular job.

15

At first sight, they might not look very similar but spiders and scorpions are close cousins. They belong to a group of arthropods called arachnids, along with tiny ticks and mites.

SPIDER SUPPER

Most spiders feed on insects, though some large species can catch birds, frogs and small mammals. Some spiders hunt their prey on the ground. Others spin sticky, silk webs to trap flying insects.

Golden orb-web spiders spin huge, silk webs, the size of bedsheets, between the trees. Spiders produce silk inside their bodies, then squeeze it out through tiny nozzles at their rear.

SPIDER BODY PLAN

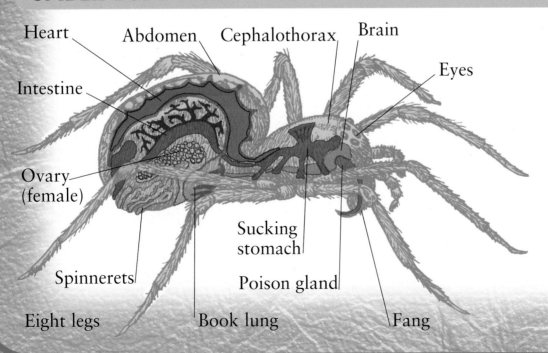

Heart   Abdomen   Cephalothorax   Brain

Eyes

Intestine

Ovary (female)

Sucking stomach

Spinnerets

Poison gland

Eight legs   Book lung   Fang

Spiders and their cousins share a similar body plan. A spider's body is divided into two parts, called the cephalothorax (head and thorax) and the abdomen. Joined to the cephalothorax are four pairs of legs. Like all arthropods, spiders have a tough exoskeleton although they do not have wings or antennae.

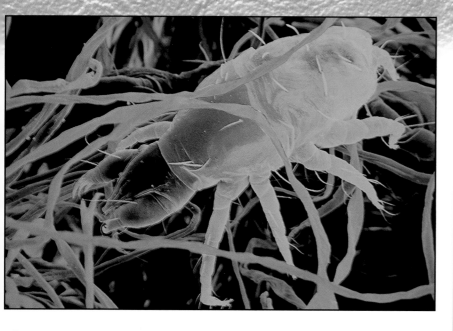

Ticks and mites are parasites. They live on other animals and plants. Most ticks and mites are tiny, but they can be dangerous. They spread diseases in animals, humans and among farmers' crops.

Amazing FACT

Horseshoe crabs live along the Atlantic coast of North America. Each spring, thousands come ashore to lay their eggs. But they are not actually crabs at all. They belong to an ancient group, closely related to the arachnids, and have hardly changed for 300 million years.

Sea-birds feed on their eggs.

SCORPION STINGS

Scorpions are secretive creatures, spending the day hiding under logs or stones. At night, they come out to hunt for food. A scorpion catches its prey in its pincer-like claws and injects it with poison from the sting in its tail. Scorpions also use their stings in self-defence.

Scorpions are well suited to living in hot, dry desert conditions. A thick, waxy coating stops them losing too much water from their bodies. They also lift their bodies off the ground to cool off.

Fish are vertebrates. They are cold-blooded and live in fresh and salty water, using gills to breathe oxygen. There are more species of fish than all other vertebrates put together. Gristly (cartilaginous) and bony fish are the two main types.

BONY FISH

Tuna, catfish, eels, seahorses and sticklebacks all belong to a group called bony fish. They have skeletons made of bone. With over 20,000 species, this group contains over 95 per cent of all fish.

The group of bony fish contains some of the most striking fish in the world. These beautifully coloured golden butterfly fish live on coral reefs.

BONY FISH BODY PLAN

Most bony fish have muscular, streamlined bodies for swimming. Fins propel the fish through the water and help it to balance. Each fin is worked by its own group of muscles, so that bony fish can steer easily.

An air-filled sac called a swim bladder allows the fish to float upright in the water. The fish's body is covered in overlapping scales for protection. A bony flap, called the operculum, covers the fish's delicate gills.

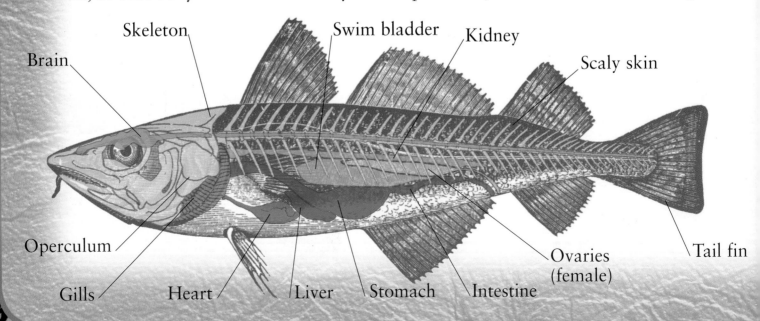

Brain — Skeleton — Swim bladder — Kidney — Scaly skin

Operculum — Gills — Heart — Liver — Stomach — Intestine — Ovaries (female) — Tail fin

SHARKS AND RAYS

Sharks, skates and rays are cartilaginous fish. This means that, instead of bone, their skeletons are made of gristly cartilage which makes them very light, flexible and strong. Cartilaginous fish use this to their advantage. Many are speedy swimmers, and fast and efficient ocean hunters.

Whale shark cruising in Australia.

Amazing FACT

The huge whale shark is the biggest fish in the sea. This giant grows over 18 metres long and weighs 20 tonnes. Despite its enormous size, the whale shark is harmless. It cruises through the water, filtering out the tiny sea animals that it eats.

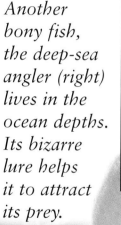

Another bony fish, the deep-sea angler (right) lives in the ocean depths. Its bizarre lure helps it to attract its prey.

Rays and other cartilaginous fish do not have swim bladders. Instead, their large, oil-filled livers are thought to help them to keep afloat.

19

Frogs and toads are cold-blooded vertebrates. Like salamanders, newts, and caecilians, they belong to the amphibian group. They spend time on land and in the water.

LIFE CYCLE OF A FROG

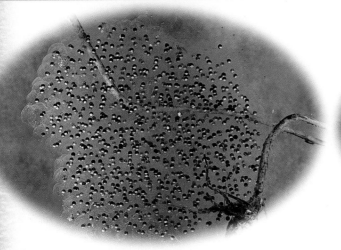

1 In spring, adult frogs return to a pond to breed. The female lays thousands of eggs, or spawn, which the male fertilizes. The eggs are covered in jelly for protection.

2 About 10 days later, the eggs hatch into tiny fish-like tadpoles with long tails for swimming. Like fish, they breathe through gills, taking in oxygen dissolved in the water.

NEWTS AND SALAMANDERS

Newts and salamanders have longer bodies than frogs and toads, shorter legs and longer tails. Some have lungs, but others breathe through their skins which must be kept moist and slimy to absorb oxygen. They tend to live in cool, shady places in or near water. All salamanders are meat-eaters, feeding on small animals, like insects, slugs and worms.

Some salamanders have poisonous or vile-tasting skins. They are often brightly coloured to deter predators. This is a European fire salamander.

Adult frogs and toads have squat bodies with long back legs for jumping, and webbed back feet for swimming. Frogs tend to have smoother skin than toads.

A tadpole-like axolotl.

Amazing FACT

The odd-looking axolotl is an amphibian that never grows up. This salamander spends its whole life as a tadpole. It needs the chemical iodine to develop, and this is not present in its natural lake habitat.

3 Over the next 12 weeks or so, the tadpoles' tails gradually shrink and they grow legs instead. They also lose their gills and develop lungs, as they turn into tiny frogs.

4 Soon they are ready to live on land. Young frogs shed their skins several times before they grow into adults. In about three years' time, they will be fully grown.

Caecilians remain hidden in their soil burrows and are rarely seen by humans. They rely on their sense of smell to find food and a mate.

CAECILIANS

With their long bodies and lack of legs, caecilians look more like giant worms than amphibians. They mostly live in the tropics, and burrow in the damp earth. They feed on earthworms and termites, using their heads as spades for digging up food. Some caecilians lay eggs, like other amphibians. But about half produce live young.

Like fish and amphibians, reptiles are cold-blooded vertebrates. But they mostly live on land where their dry, scaly skins help to stop their bodies from drying out. Most reptiles lay eggs, protected by tough shells.

SNAPPING JAWS

Reptiles range from tiny lizards to enormous crocodiles. Crocodiles and alligators are fierce predators. Their long snouts are lined with sharp teeth for grabbing prey and their bodies are covered in armour-plating.

Crocodiles are well suited to life in the water where they hunt. They use their powerful tails to leap up and grab prey.

Amazing FACT

The awesome dinosaurs were an ancient group of reptiles. They first appeared about 230 million years ago and dominated life on Earth for over 160 million years. Reptiles, such as plesiosaurs and pterosaurs, also ruled the prehistoric seas and skies.

Dinosaur literally means a 'terrible lizard'.

All snakes share a similar shape, with a long, slender body and no legs or limbs. This snaky shape is ideal for slithering, climbing, swimming and burrowing through soil or sand. This means that snakes can live in a wide range of habitats.

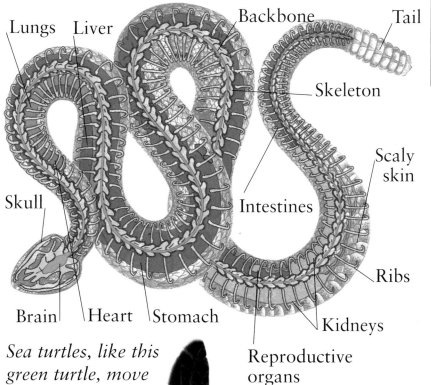

Lungs   Liver   Backbone   Tail

Skeleton

Skull

Scaly skin

Intestines

Ribs

Brain   Heart   Stomach

Kidneys

Reproductive organs

Sea turtles, like this green turtle, move clumsily on land but are graceful swimmers. Their front legs act like flippers to propel them along.

Scientists think that snakes developed from two-legged lizard ancestors. Today's lizards range from tiny geckos (above) to the impressive 3-metre-long Komodo dragon.

TURTLE SHELLS

Turtles and tortoises are easy to identify because of their box-like shells. These are made up of bony plates, covered in a tough material called keratin. For protection, turtles and tortoises can pull their heads and limbs inside their shells.

Scientists think that birds evolved from small dinosaurs. Gradually, they developed feathers instead of scales, beaks instead of jaws, and their front limbs became wings. Birds are warm-blooded vertebrates. Like reptiles, they use lungs to breathe oxygen from the air.

A fossil of Archaeopteryx, or 'ancient wings', the first bird to live on Earth about 150 million years ago. It was about the size of a crow.

EGGS AND NESTS

All birds lay eggs with hard shells, so most birds build nests to provide a safe place for their eggs and young. The eggs need to be kept warm for the chicks to develop. Usually, the female sits on them.

This grebe is incubating her eggs. Most birds also look after their chicks.

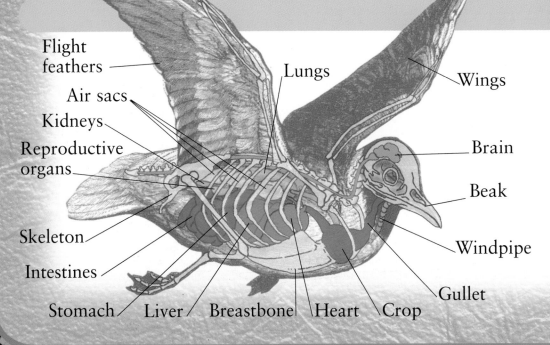

Flight feathers
Air sacs
Kidneys
Reproductive organs
Skeleton
Intestines
Stomach
Liver
Breastbone
Heart
Crop
Gullet
Windpipe
Beak
Brain
Wings
Lungs

BUILT FOR FLIGHT

Most birds are designed for flight. Flying birds all share the same streamlined body shape. Their bones are hollow to reduce weight and their front limbs have become wings. The power needed for flight is provided by massive chest muscles, that are fixed to a large breastbone.

Penguins cannot fly but are fast and efficient swimmers. They use their wings as flippers to chase through the water in search of fish to eat.

FLIGHTLESS BIRDS

Over millions of years, some birds have lost the power of flight. Some flightless birds, such as kiwis and kakapos, live on remote islands, safe from predators. They do not need to be able to fly to escape from danger. Others, such as ostriches, are too heavy to fly but can run very fast on their long legs instead.

Amazing FACT

The bee humingbird from Cuba is the world's smallest bird. A male weighs as little as 1.6 g and measures just 57 mm long, half of which is made up of its beak and tail. Incredibly, these tiny birds are smaller than many of the moths and butterflies that share their rainforest home.

Bee hummingbird.

25

Amazing mammals include a wide range of creatures, from enormous whales and elephants, to tiny mice and shrews. It is also the group to which human beings belong. Mammals are warm-blooded vertebrates that breathe air through lungs.

LOOKING AFTER BABY

Most mammals are placental mammals. A baby grows inside the mother and is nourished by her placenta. When born, it looks like a tiny version of its parents. All mammals feed their young on milk.

Apes, monkeys and humans belong to a group of mammals called primates. The two species of chimpanzee are our closest living relatives. They are more closely related to us than they are to orang-utans (above).

MAMMAL BODY PLAN

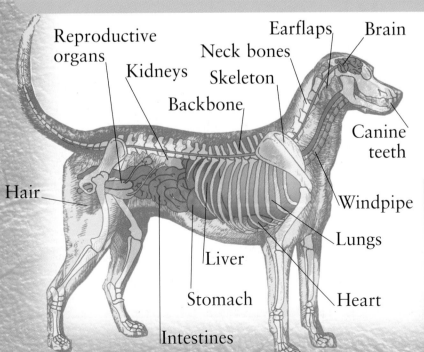

Reproductive organs
Kidneys
Hair
Liver
Stomach
Intestines
Neck bones
Skeleton
Backbone
Earflaps
Brain
Canine teeth
Windpipe
Lungs
Heart

All mammals share some characteristics in common. They are vertebrates, with seven bones in their necks. They are the only animals with true hair and earflaps which direct sounds into their ears. Different mammals have specialised teeth suited to their particular diet.

Aardvarks feed on ants and termites.

Amazing FACT

The blue whale is the biggest mammal, and the largest animal that has ever lived. An adult can grow up to 33 m long and weigh up to 130 tonnes. A blue whale's heart alone is the size of a car.

Blue whales can dive 200 m deep.

FIRST MAMMALS

About 250 million years ago, reptiles were the main land animals. Gradually, some began to develop into mammals. The first true mammals appeared on Earth about 220 million years ago. They were small and looked like rats or shrews. It was only when the dinosaurs died out, about 65 million years ago, that mammals took over.

Some mammals can glide but bats are the only mammals capable of real, flapping flight.

The biggest mammal on land is the African elephant. Males can weigh up to 10 tonnes and stand 4 m tall.

27

Not all mammals give birth to well-formed babies, like the placental mammals. Two groups, called the monotremes and marsupials, have different ways of reproducing. Monotremes are mammals that lay eggs, while marsupials have pouches.

MAMMALS WITH POUCHES

Kangaroos, koalas and wallabies are marsupials. These mammals produce young which are blind, weak and underdeveloped. Despite this, the tiny baby crawls up its mother's fur to her pouch. Here it feeds on milk and grows until it is strong enough to survive outside.

A joey, or baby kangaroo, peeks out of its mother's pouch. Even when it is quite grown up, it hops back into her pouch for safety.

Koalas depend on eucalyptus trees.

EGG-LAYING MAMMALS

Three extraordinary species of mammals – the duck-billed platypus, and the long-beaked and short-beaked echidnas – belong to the group of monotremes. They are found in Australia and New Guinea. Unusually, these mammals lay soft-shelled eggs. But, like other mammals, the females suckle their young on milk when they hatch. Duck-billed platypuses lay their eggs in a nest in a riverbank tunnel.

American opposums (left) have as many as 20 babies in a litter. It gets very crowded inside their mother's pouch so some of the babies ride on her back.

Echidnas (right) eat insects and earthworms. They have narrow snouts to poke around and sniff out food. Then they lap it up with their long, sticky tongues.

The duck-billed platypus forages underwater for freshwater insects and other invertebrates. It has webbed feet for swimming and uses its wide, duck-like bill to feel around for food.

29

Mammals

• With about 1750 species, rodents are the largest group of mammals, while the aardvark is the only species in its group.

Birds

• The world's rarest bird may be the Spix's macaw from Brazil. There may be only one surviving male left in the wild and another 30 in captivity. Trapping for the pet trade and habitat destruction have endangered these birds.

Reptiles

• Tortoises can be very long-lived. One male Marion's tortoise lived for over 152 years.

Amphibians

• The world's smallest frog, the tiny Cuban frog, would fit on your thumbnail. Yet the African goliath frog is 30 times as long.

Fish

• The largest predatory fish is the great white shark. Despite its man-eating reputation though, it very rarely attacks humans.

Insects

• The most dangerous animal in the world is a blood-sucking insect, the mosquito. It spreads the deadly disease malaria which kills humans.

Arachnids

• Some spiders catch their prey by spitting fast-setting glue at them to make them unable to move and stop them from escaping. These spiders also spit at their enemies and rival spiders.

Molluscs

• The African giant snail is the biggest snail on land. With its head and tail stretched out, it would fit across these two pages.

GLOSSARY

adapted
Having skills or features which help an animal, plant or person to survive in a particular place.

antennae
Feelers on an animal's head which help it to touch and sense things.

cold-blooded
Animals which cannot control their own body temperature.

exoskeleton
An invertebrate's tough, outer coating around its soft body.

gills
Thin, feathery body parts which fish and tadpoles use to breathe.

incubate
The way in which birds sit on their eggs to keep them warm.

metamorphosis
The changes which take place in an insect's or amphibian's body as it develops into an adult.

parasites
Animals which live on or in other animals or plants and get their nourishment from them.

photosynthesis
The way in which plants make their own food from carbon dioxide and water, using energy from sunlight.

placenta
Part of a female mammal's body which nourishes her growing baby and provides it with oxygen.

species
A group of living things that have similar features.

taxonomy
How scientists divide animals into groups, based upon their shared features. Also called classification.

warm-blooded
Animals that can control their own body temperature, enabling them to be active in the heat or cold.

31